Quilt

of

Many Verses

Daryl Langworthy

ISBN 979-8-89345-469-7 (paperback)
ISBN 979-8-89345-470-3 (digital)

Copyright © 2024 by Daryl Langworthy

All rights reserved. No part of this publication may be reproduced, distributed, or transmitted in any form or by any means, including photocopying, recording, or other electronic or mechanical methods without the prior written permission of the publisher. For permission requests, solicit the publisher via the address below.

Christian Faith Publishing
832 Park Avenue
Meadville, PA 16335
www.christianfaithpublishing.com

Printed in the United States of America

Ye have not, because Ye ask not.
—James 3:18

It is more blessed to give than to receive.
—Acts 20:25

You shall Love your neighbor as yourself.
—Romans 13:9

Submit yourself to God. Resist the devil, and he will flee.
—James 4:1

If you honor God; he will Honor You.
—1 Samuel 2:30

For me to live is Christ, and to die is gain.
—Philippians 1:21

In God I put my trust:
I will not be afraid what man can do to me.
—Psalms 56:11

Thy Kingdom come. Thy will be done on earth as it is in heaven.
—Matthew 6:10

Contents

Introduction	vii
Our Home in Heaven	1
Be Faithful	2
Knowledge	4
Don't Worry, Be Hopeful	5
Purpose	6
Let Go and Let God	7
Strengths from Grace	8
Walk by Faith	9
Peace	10
Prayer	11
Freedom in Christ	12
The Awful Tongue	13
Finding Christ	14
Death	15
Good	17

Introduction

This writing is a patchwork of spiritual truths. Knowledge of God and His words.

Many verses used are from the King James Version of the Bible and words of wisdom to live every day learned from years of radio bible studies.

Learn from our home on Earth, so we can graduate to our eternal heavenly home.

Our assurance of this comes from knowing the truths of God. All truths are in the Bible. In this world, turn to the Lord. He declares us guiltless. No one can separate us from the love of God.

Be assured of your faith in Christ. If your heart is right with God, you can be confident in your position with him.

Ask questions in prayers, and God will guide us. Whatever we ask, God will answer with—yes or no or wait (Daniel 9:17–22).

One of the most important things we can do in this life is keep His commandments and live in His will Exodus 20:2–17.

God's word gives us:

> Security. We thrive when we trust God's word.
> Identity. Who we are controls our behavior.
> Belong. Who wants me (community).
> Purpose. Serve
> Competence. To fulfill my purpose.

By reading and hearing the word, it will guide you in being who you were created to be.

Our Home in Heaven

❖

It is not our works; it is the gospel that saves us. Believe in the gospel. Keep rules to "love one another."

Be born again by the power of the Holy Spirit. We are in Christ. Christ is in us. Through the redemption of Jesus Christ, we know God. He spiritually abides in us. God has a good sense of humor. Learn to love where you live. Go wherever He calls you. Move toward God, even when it's not comfortable. Be a disciple of God. Live with purpose. The more you risk for the Lord, the more He protects us. We make mistakes. Don't be afraid. It's okay to make mistakes. Leave your fear with God. We have the natural desire to be led astray. We have so many empty things in our lives today.

The fall (Adam and Eve) changed our being. Because of the fall, the desires of the heart have been sinful.

Damnation of our souls by sinning dulls our minds to the Lord. Don't settle for too little. Reclaim what God wants for us. The promises of God are great.

Walk by the spirit and you will not satisfy the flesh (sin). Turn away from legalism (earthly ways). Seek Jesus's way.

Be Faithful

◈

Stay in the Bible. Seek the Lord and don't let evil into your life. Stay close to the word and don't get caught up in "dead deeds."

Jesus died for us to save us and to do good works. Don't think you have to do good work to be saved. We are guilty and need to hear warnings. Stay away from idols.

False religion—don't worship idols. Follow only God and don't turn your back on Him.

Pride is the original sin. Don't be prideful. God will judge the prideful.

God allows sin to follow its natural course. Don't be a sinner. Sin brings death, not the joy of heaven's eternity. Justice has come. Jesus is justice. Be patient. God will get vengeance for those who persecute Christians. God says, "Vengeance is mine. I will repay, saith the Lord" (Romans 12:19–21).

Will you meet Jesus as a friend or judge? God sent His Son Jesus to save us. No one is good enough. Gift is on the table…pick it up. Choose Jesus and lay your sin on the cross. Don't leave an offer on the table. Give Him what is left of your life. Restore your life through obedience to His word.

Acknowledge the Lord of our life. We are challenging children of God, but He loves and forgives us.

Don't get caught up in cultural Christianity but real Christianity from God through the Bible. He is the Prince of Peace. His ways will not always be our ways.

In this world, we will have tribulations, but He will overcome the world. Make every effort to enter the narrow door. The door is going to be hard to get in, and one day will be closed. Everyone needs repentance.

Don't miss this opportunity while the door is open. God is patient with us.

Knowledge

Narrow is the road to the gate to heaven. Don't be one who stands outside pleading and begging. God says, "I don't know you" (Matthew 7:21–23, 25:11–12).

Go out and help others to find the door. Put honor and truth in front of comfort.

Seek to be honorable, and pray for our leaders to act with honor. Don't seek power, it will lead you astray.

In our world policies today, we need to seek duty, honor, and country. Regain faith, have hope, and build your honor. Be courageous, not timid.

Have a sweet spirit, bury old arguments, and move on. Be a role model. Whatever comes out of our mouth, let it be kind. Look for places to overcome difficulties. Pray for solutions.

Adversity promotes the gospel. Read about Paul's imprisonment that helped him promote the Bible (Philippians 1:12).

We serve a God who can do the impossible. Don't be trapped in your way of thinking. Lead with your strengths. Confidence is the ability you need to live the way you are wired. We are all wired to thrive in Christ.

Be a leader. We have a great responsibility to teach the Bible and Jesus. In your heart, make room for Jesus. He was rich and became poor so that we may become rich (birth of Jesus) (Luke 2:7–20).

Jesus is Lord. Glory to God in the highest.

Don't Worry, Be Hopeful

We are God's family. God is the vine, and we are the branches. Everyone has a part in God's family. Everyone has a job to do in life. Examples are teaching, serving, laboring, and producing. All jobs are equally important. Love where you are at.

Make sure to be around people who believe and who don't gossip. Be peaceful with all men and follow holiness.

Put off your old self and put on new. Put off falsehood and speak truthfully to our neighbors. Work to give not to get rich but to be able to give to others.

Get rid of all bitterness. Be kind and compassionate to one another as God gives to us.

Share the good news of Jesus. Walk with God and connect with people. We can impact the world as we mature as a disciple of Christ. Tie yourself to Jesus and not man. Be under the headship of Jesus, not Adam (Man).

Everything is under God's control call out to him. His ways are greater than ours (Isaiah 55:9).

As long as there is breathe, there is hope. Learn to be content, "I can do all things in Christ" (Philippians 4:13).

Purpose

We have the assurance that we will be in heaven when we die because we know Jesus died for our sins. We gain a sense of confidence when we know God.

We have salvation through our walk with Jesus. We have a new nature not to sin. Whoever has Jesus has eternal life. We have the blessed holy spirit of God when we understand the message of Jesus.

Our children value relationships, not stuff. Christmas is the month of Christology—all about Jesus. Christmas is not about presents but about God's presence in us.

> The greatest gift of Christmas, for God so loved the world that he gave his only begotten son, that whosoever believeth in him should not perish, but have everlasting life. (John 3:16)

> Christmas (Birth of Jesus) is the promise. Easter (Resurrection of Jesus) is the fulfillment. (John 11:25–26)

God provides what we need if we trust in him, not what we think we want and need. Stay in the will of God.

Let Go and Let God

When we wear the helmet of salvation, we belong to God, and the devil will flee.

The holy spirit of God brings us calmness. Have a strong mind and know that Jesus is stronger than our doubts.

Run from desires and pleasures. God is the true source of our happiness. Trust in the word and listen to the Holy Spirit. He brings focus and rest in God's word.

The heart is deceitful. Don't sin against God. He pours blessings upon us. Trust in the Lord with all your heart.

We think we know better than God, but we don't. Submit to His authority. Protect your mind from distractions. God is always shaping us. The grace and peace of God change things we think about.

Don't worry; worry shows a lack of faith. He can make you what you don't think you are.

Be doers of the word; not just readers of the word. If he calls you, he will equip you.

There is no greater power than being in harmony with oneself. Know that you are part of the divine. God is "I am," not "I was," or "I will," but "I am" (John 14:6).

Live for today only. We have large windshields for looking forward. Don't get distracted by looking in rearview mirror, looking back.

Strengths from Grace

Don't lay up riches for yourself, but be rich toward God. "Seek ye the kingdom of God and all these things shall be added to you" (Matthew 6:33).

> Beware of covetousness. A man's life consists not in the abundance of things he posseseth. (Luke 12:15–21, 31–34)

Believe, receive, and become a child of God (free gift of grace). Believe no matter what.

Come to Jesus in your unbelief, and He will protect us. We will never be regretful for being courageous for God. Don't set boundaries on God's grace. God created you to be great.

There is nothing that you can do to make God love you more or less. God is love.

Don't fear sin. Sin abounds, but we must put on the armor of God. Jesus casts out demons.

God is always working in your life. He will guide you and keep you his number 1.

God is Trinity, three in one, Father, Son, and Holy Spirit (coequal parts). Jesus is both God and man equal to the Father.

The joy of the Lord is our strength. The Lord is our provider. Make a choice to rejoice.

Pursue God always for eternal life. Let me not be ashamed of my hope (Psalms 119:116).

Walk by Faith

❖

> Now faith is the substance of things hoped for, the evidence of things not seen.
>
> —Hebrews 11:1

Don't be a slave to sin. Have confidence that you are saved from sin's power.

You were lost, now you are found (saved) (Luke 15:10–24).

> Keep your life from the love of money, and be content with what you have, for he has said; "I will never leave you nor forsake you." (Hebrews 13:5)

God is the potter, and we are the clay. We are put through fire so we come out as gold.

Jesus is the wonderful counselor, who leads us and guides us to all truths through the holy spirit (Isaiah 9:6–7)

No longer be defined by what has happened to you. Reprogram your mind to think differently.

Reading the word of God cleanses the mind. Exist to worship God, not people. Hear the gospel every day.

Peace

❖

Your mind shapes your life. Your mind is connected to God. Transform your mind.

He who meditates day and night prospers. Learn to meditate on God and good.

Discipline your mind for meditation. Pray for a meditative mind, discipline of silence and solitude.

Hearken to God's word. Read the gospels (good news). God sent His Son to save us.

Give God a chance. Try Him on—He fits!

True faith holds fast. Stand in Christ always.

When we know that we are walking with God, we are at peace. Think of things that are noble, worthy, pure, and lovely. Go and do this for the peace of God.

> Don't worry about anything, pray about everything. (Philippines 4:6–7)

Ask yourself when making decisions, Will this glorify God? Will my choices be a good influence on others? Make sure to help others for God, not for yourself.

Treat each other with tenderness. The Lord wants peace, harmony, and contentment. We are one body in Christ.

Prayer

Seek God and not the world. Pray God will open the door. Desire the will of God.

> Honor God and He will honor you. (1 Samuel 2:30)

Pray for God's wisdom. Pray for people. There is hope in the grace of Jesus. Grace can change hearts. Grace can change a person completely. Grace can make saints out of sinners. Your mother's prayers have followed you.

Stay *gold* (strong, solid). Don't let the world soften you. God started a good work in us, and He will complete it. We are destined for victory (Deuteronomy 20:4).

Pray through the scriptures, and answers will come. Instead of telling someone their wrongs, tell them I am praying for you. Jesus is praying for our unity and oneness.

Keep praying for people, the lost sheep, and rebellious people. They are not beyond God's reach. Be a praying person, not a nag. Tell sinner I have always acted in your best interest. I hope you will treat me the same.

Lord shows us the gospel and rescues us out of stupidity. Trust the Lord with all thine heart and lean not unto thine own understanding (Proverbs 3:5–6).

Freedom in Christ

Don't sin. It takes the joy out of life. One cannot live in bitterness and serve God.

Pray for the sinner. Confess your faults one to another, that ye may be healed (James 5:16).

Cover my children in a quilt of prayers. Let them learn freedom in Christ by learning these concepts: Be saved, be sanctified (move toward God), be filled with the Holy Spirit, be thankful always, be submissive (humble yourself), be willing to suffer, be supportive, and be free.

Have a strong mind and know that Jesus is stronger than our doubts. Grow from weakness to strength in God. My fruit is better than gold (Proverbs 8:10–19).

The Awful Tongue

It is better to be told a hard truth by a friend than to be flattered by an enemy. Bridle our tongue. Whenever we open our lips, let it be kind. Speak only with grace, seasoned with salt (Colossians 4:6).

As we are on our journey, we should look around and observe those around us, helping those in need and ministering God's love and acceptance to them all.

Our tongue can be positive and do good or a fire that corrupts the body. "But the tongue can no man tame; it is an unruly evil, full of deadly poison (James 3:8).

Learn to listen, not talk. We have two ears and one tongue. Listening is a lost art.

Silence is a powerful communicator.

Finding Christ

We need to find Christ. Our hearts have no meaning until it rests in Christ. The world cannot provide meaning, only God (Isaiah 26:4).

We don't know the plan for tomorrow. Take each day as it comes. Take today's step with God and don't worry about tomorrow.

Be in the world and not of it. Learn how to live holy in an unholy world. It's about who you are, not what you have.

Society's acceptance does not help fill the hole in our hearts. God is the only thing that works. Make God first, not second or third. Invite Him into everything; He will guide.

Our country is based on a spiritual foundation. Learn and teach our great American story. Evangelism begins in our families, neighborhoods, and churches.

Love and serve our neighbors.

Death

I will be defined by the joy of Jesus in my heart. Our behavior is a choice. Make wise choices. If you choose to do wrong, you will suffer the consequences.

You treasure what is earned, not what is given to you. Submit your life to Jesus Christ. God gave us His spirit to open our souls.

Wait on God. Be willing to wait for God. Wait for God and keep His way, and He will exalt you. An example is David who waited for God as he was being pursued by Saul for ten years.

Many people lost their blessings because they didn't wait for God. Learn to share your life with meaningful goals for commitment to spiritual growth. We are restless with an aching deep in our souls. Seek Jesus, only He can fill the hole in our hearts. Empty relationships will never satisfy the void in us, the longing for something more. Let Jesus live in your heart; He is the only one who can bring satisfaction to your heart (Psalms 22:23–26).

Run with patience, the race he has set before us (Hebrews 12:1). The more we fall in love with Jesus, and fellowship with others who will give growth to you.

We were created from dust and will return to dust. Cremation is as burial. All bodies return to dust. God will give us new glorified bodies no matter how we die. Fire will not separate us from resurrection (many Christians were burned at the stake).

The Bible is silent on burial procedures. Cremation is a choice. As Christians, we are at liberty to make a choice. One day we will be resurrected from the grave (eternal hope).

In battles, men are burned, drowned, and eaten up. Soul resurrection will happen no matter how we get buried. God brings together whatever has been scattered. God will gather His beloved (Mark 13:27).

Believe in the word and live by God's commandments. Love God with all thy soul and love thy neighbor as thyself (Mark 12:29–31).

Good

❖

Good things happen to people that deepen their relationship with God.

We have seen through thousands of years nations rise and fall. Our hope is in Christ. I have been young, and now I am old. I have learned to fret not (Psalms 35:25).

Look beyond earthly views and know God is sufficient. Put your trust in Him. He isn't finished. He is in charge, and the wicked will be no more (Psalms 37:34–40).

His word and scriptures are the lamp unto our feet (Psalms 119:105). He has given us this gift. Now we know how to live abundantly.

Pursue God. A life without Him is really no life at all. Grace and peace be multiplied to you through the knowledge of God and of Jesus our Lord (2 Peter 1:2).

This writing is a quick read on encouraging verses from the Bible. Delight in the Lord by learning His word.

> O Earth, Earth, Earth, hear the word of the Lord. (Jeremiah 22:29)